REMARKABLE CANADIANS

Terry Fox

by Bryan Pezzi

Published by Weigl Educational Publishers Limited
6325 – 10 Street SE
Calgary, Alberta, Canada
T2H 2Z9

Web site: www.weigl.ca

All of the Internet URLs given in the book were valid at the time of publication. However,
due to the dynamic nature of the Internet, some addresses may have changed, or sites
may have ceased to exist since publication. While the author and publisher regret any
inconvenience this may cause readers, no responsibility for any such changes can be accepted
by either the author or the publisher.

Library and Archives Canada Cataloguing in Publication

Pezzi, Bryan
    Terry Fox / Bryan Pezzi.

(Remarkable Canadians)
Includes index.
ISBN 1-55388-207-5 (bound).--ISBN 1-55388-211-3 (pbk.)
    1. Fox, Terry, 1958-1981--Juvenile literature. 2. Cancer--Patients--
Canada--Biography. 3. Runners (Sports)--Canada--Biography. I.Title.
II. Series.

RC265.6.F68P49 2006   j362.196'994'0092   C2006-900922-8

Printed in the United States of America
1 2 3 4 5 6 7 8 9 0 10 09 08 07 06

Editor: Heather C. Hudak
Design: Terry Paulhus

We acknowledge the financial support of the Government of Canada through the Book
Publishing Industry Development Program (BPIDP) for our publishing activities.

Cover: Terrence Stanley Fox died of cancer before his 23rd birthday. During his short life,
Terry inspired people around the world to fight cancer. Since Terry Fox's death, the Terry Fox
Foundation has raised millions of dollars for cancer research.

Photograph Credits
Cover: CP; CP: pages 5, 8, 18; CP (Bill Becker): pages 1, 10, 20; CP (Don Denton): page 6; CP
(Jeremy Gilbert): page 16; CP (Jonathan Hayward): page 13 TL; CP (Ian Scott): page 13 TR;
CP (Chuck Stoody): page 14; CP (Tannis Toohey): page 15; CP (Sean Vokey): page 19;
Copyright © Province of British of Columbia. All rights reserved. Reprinted with permission
of the Province of British Columbia. www.ipp.gov.bc.ca: page 7 top left.

Every reasonable effort has been made to trace ownership and to obtain permission to reprint
copyright material. The publishers would be pleased to have any errors or omissions brought
to their attention so that they may be corrected in subsequent printings.

Contents

Who Is Terry Fox?

Terry Fox is a symbol of hope for many Canadians. When Terry was 18 years old, he lost his leg to bone cancer. Terry decided he wanted to help find a cure for cancer. Three years later, in 1980, he began to run across Canada. Canadians were inspired by Terry's efforts, and they gave money for cancer research. Terry's disease took his life in 1981, but his memory lives on. Every September, the Terry Fox Run takes place in cities throughout Canada and the world. In places as far away as China and Turkey, people continue Terry's work. They run, hoping to put an end to cancer.

"I've got to be positive. I've got all of Canada looking at me."

Growing Up

Terry Fox was born in Winnipeg, Manitoba, on July 28, 1958. He was the second child of Rolly and Betty Fox. Terry had an older brother named Fred. He also had a younger brother and a younger sister. They were named Darrell and Judith. In 1968, the family moved to Port Coquitlam, a town outside Vancouver, British Columbia.

Terry was a patient and energetic child. Once he started something, Terry did not give up. He could spend hours playing games. At school, Terry worked hard to achieve his goals. Terry never liked to miss a day of school.

🍁 Today, more than 50,000 people live in Port Coquitlam.

British Columbia Tidbits

COAT OF ARMS

TREE
Western Red Cedar

FLOWER
Pacific Dogwood

British Columbia makes up about 10 per cent of Canada's land.

Almost one-third of Canada's fresh water is in British Columbia.

The highest point in British Columbia is Mount Fairweather. It is 4,663 metres high.

More than 4 million people live in British Columbia.

Victoria, the capital city of British Columbia, is located on Vancouver Island.

Think about it!

Research Port Coquitlam and locate it on a map. What major city is Port Coquitlam nearest? How do you think growing up in Port Coquitlam might have influenced Terry?

Practice Makes Perfect

Terry played many sports in school. He took up baseball, rugby, and cross-country running. Terry worked hard at every sport. More than anything, Terry wanted to play basketball. He worked hard to improve his skills. Soon, Terry was good enough to play on his school's basketball team. After high school, Terry enrolled at Simon Fraser University. He studied **kinesiology** and played on the university basketball team. Terry wanted to become a high school gym teacher.

In March 1977, Terry felt pain in his right knee. He went to the hospital to find out what was wrong. Tests showed that Terry had bone cancer. The doctors told him that they needed to remove his leg. Terry's right leg was **amputated** 15 centimetres above the knee. The months ahead were difficult.

🍁 After losing his leg, Terry ran in a marathon. He trained for seven months before entering the race.

Terry learned to walk with a **prosthetic** leg. He also received **chemotherapy** treatments at a cancer clinic. Terry's hair fell out, and he felt sick because of the treatment. At the cancer clinic, Terry saw many people suffering. That's when Terry decided to run across Canada and raise money for cancer research.

When he felt strong enough, Terry began to train. He began running every day, using his prosthetic leg. After a few months, Terry was able to run several kilometres. He entered a **marathon** in Prince George, British Columbia. Terry came in last place, but he was proud to cross the finish line. He returned home and told his family he wanted to run across Canada.

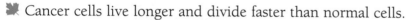
Cancer cells live longer and divide faster than normal cells.

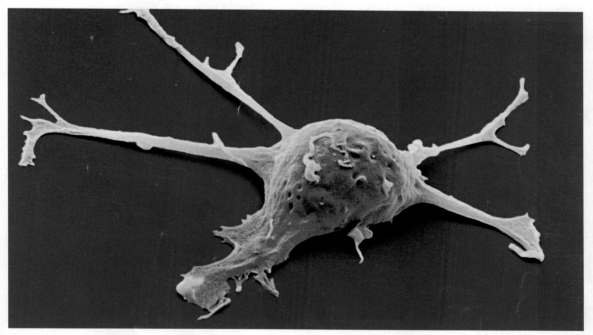

Key Events

Terry's Marathon of Hope began on April 12, 1980. It was a cold and windy day in St. John's, Newfoundland. Terry dipped his **artificial** leg in the Atlantic Ocean to mark the beginning of his run. Terry was joined by his friend Doug Alward. Doug drove alongside Terry in a van that had been donated to them. Along the way, people saw what Terry was doing. Some people provided meals for Terry and Doug. Others made **donations** for cancer research.

At first, few people knew about Terry's Marathon of Hope. As he travelled across the country, more people took notice. Along the way, Terry made speeches, attended events, and gave interviews. By the time he reached Toronto, Terry was welcomed as a hero. He ran to Nathan Phillips Square at Toronto's city hall. More than 10,000 people greeted him there. Toronto Maple Leafs captain Darryl Sittler presented Terry with a National Hockey League (NHL) jersey. That day, Terry raised $100,000 to fight cancer.

🍁 Terry Fox has inspired many people, including athletes. Darryl Sittler said, "I've been around athletes a long time and I've never seen any with his courage."

Thoughts from Terry

Terry has spoken about the key events that have shaped his life. Here are some examples.

Terry worries that he might not be able to complete the Marathon of Hope.

"...if I don't make it, the Marathon of Hope better continue.... It's got to go on without me."

Terry loses his hair during chemotherapy treatment.

"I cried and got upset for a longer time when they told me I was going to lose my hair than when they told me I was going to lose my leg."

Terry has to stop running in Thunder Bay, Ontario, when cancer spreads to his lungs.

"I just hope that I have been an **inspiration** to others.... I will not give up."

Terry Fox's letter to the Canadian Cancer Society

"I'm not a dreamer, and I'm not saying that this will initiate any kind of definite answer or cure to cancer, but I believe in miracles. I have to."

Terry speaks to cheering crowds in Toronto. He wants people to give money for cancer research.

"If you've given a dollar, you are part of the Marathon of Hope."

Terry's speech in Scarborough, Ontario.

"I'm not doing this to become rich or famous...To me, being famous is not the idea of the run. The only important part is that cancer can be beaten."

What Is a Health Hero?

There are many ways to help people suffering from cancer and other diseases. Scientists research ways to cure illness. Doctors treat people who are sick. Care workers help people who live with disease. Terry Fox made a difference by raising money for cancer research. He inspired other people to do the same. The people on the next page are other Canadian health heroes who have raised money for medical research.

🍁 Canada is one of the few countries in the world that provides free health care to citizens who cannot afford to pay for it.

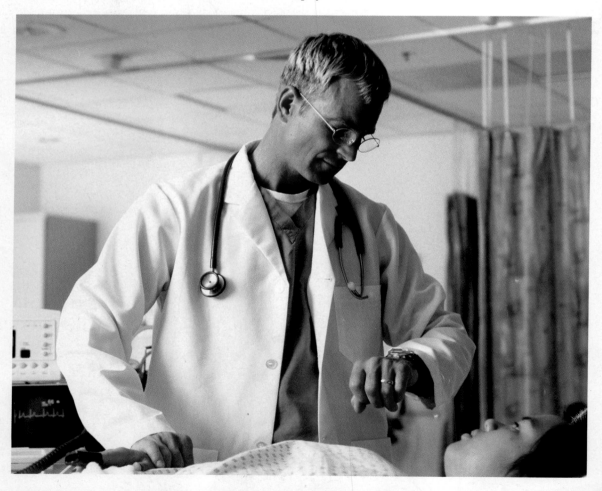

Health Heroes 101

Rick Hansen (1957–)

Cause Spinal cord injuries
Achievements Rick Hansen was a friend of Terry Fox. They played wheelchair basketball together. When Hansen was 15 years old, a car crash left him in a wheelchair. In 1985, Hansen began his Man in Motion tour. He rode his wheelchair through 34 countries around the world. The tour lasted 792 days. Man in Motion raised $20 million to help people with **spinal cord** injuries.

Michael J. Fox (1961–)

Cause Parkinson's disease
Achievements Michael J. Fox was born in Edmonton, Alberta, and had his first professional acting role when he was just 15. After moving to Hollywood, he became a popular actor on television series such a *Family Ties* and *Spin City*. He also acted in movies, such as *Back to the Future*. Then, when he was 30 years old, he was diagnosed with **Parkinson's disease**. He took fewer acting roles and focussed on raising funds for research for a cure for Parkinson's disease. The Michael J. Fox Foundation for Parkinson's Research has raised millions of dollars since it began in 2000.

Steve Fonyo (1965–)

Cause Cancer research
Achievements Like Terry Fox, Steve Fonyo lost a leg to bone cancer. Fonyo was inspired by Terry's Marathon of Hope. In 1984, Fonyo ran across Canada to raise money for cancer research. He called his run the Journey for Lives. He made it all the way from St. John's, Newfoundland, to Victoria, British Columbia. The run raised about $13 million.

Prosthetic Limbs
A prosthesis is an artificial body part. A prosthetic limb replaces an arm or leg that has been lost to disease or injury. In the past, prosthetics were heavy and did not bend. Today's prosthetics are made from lightweight materials, such as **fibreglass**. They can bend, and they have joints that make movement more natural.

Influences

When Terry became ill, he worried that he would have to give up playing sports. The night before his operation, Terry received a visit from his high school coach. The coach showed Terry a magazine article. It was about a one-legged marathon runner named Dick Traum. Dick lost his leg at age 24, when he was hit by a car. Dick began running on his artificial leg and ran in the New York Marathon. Terry was inspired by Dick's story. He knew that he would be able to run in a marathon, too.

❦ Betty and Rolly Fox, Terry's parents, supported Terry during his battle against cancer and his Marathon of Hope run.

As soon as Terry was well enough, he wanted to play sports again. He began to meet some athletes who had **disabilities**. Terry met Rick Hansen, a wheelchair basketball player. Rick asked if Terry wanted to play on his team, the Cablecars. Terry became a skilled wheelchair basketball player. He would show up for practice, even when he felt sick from chemotherapy. Terry gained strength and confidence. His experience with disabled athletes gave Terry the courage to try to run across Canada.

The Rick Hansen Man In Motion Foundation has raised more than $178 million for spinal cord injury programs and research in Canada.

THE MARATHON

A marathon takes hours to complete. A runner prepares for a marathon by training for several months in advance. The first marathon race took place in the 1896 Olympics. Today, marathons are held in cities across Canada and around the world.

Overcoming Obstacles

Terry faced many **obstacles** in his life. Those obstacles made him try harder. Running across Canada was a huge challenge. The run would take him from St. John's, Newfoundland to Port Renfrew, British Columbia. It was an incredible journey of 8,530 km. That was like running 200 marathons in a row. Terry continued training. He trained for 3 years before starting the Marathon of Hope in 1980. Running on an artificial leg was difficult and painful. Terry ran through cold rain and fierce heat. Every day, he covered about 40 km.

Terry was running near Thunder Bay, Ontario, when his health changed. He began to cough. Then he developed a pain in his chest. Terry could not run any farther. He had to be driven to a hospital. Tests showed that Terry's cancer had reached his lungs. Terry had to end his run and return home.

🍁 During the Marathon of Hope, Terry's friend Doug would drive ahead a kilometre, then wait until Terry caught up. Then he would drive another kilometre.

Although Terry's Marathon of Hope had ended, Canadians continued to give money. All over the country, people raised money for cancer research. They were touched by Terry's struggle, and they wanted to help. By February 1981, Terry's run had raised more than $24 million. Terry reached his goal of raising one dollar for every person in Canada.

🍁 Thousands of people in Cuba took part in the Terry Fox Run in 2006, 25 years after Terry's death.

Achievements and Successes

Terry battled his disease for 10 months after he stopped running. People across the country wrote him letters and sent messages of support. Everyone wanted Terry to get well.

Terry received some important awards for his fight against cancer. On September 19, 1980, he became a Companion of the Order of Canada. This is one of the highest awards anyone in Canada can receive. However, Terry was not well enough to travel to Ottawa for an award ceremony.

Governor General Edward Schreyer presented Terry with the Order of Canada.

Instead, a ceremony was held in Terry's home town of Port Coquitlam. Terry was the youngest person ever to receive this award. He also won the Order of the Dogwood. This is a major **award** in British Columbia.

Terry died on June 28, 1981. It was a month before his 23rd birthday. There was a large **funeral** for Terry, which aired on national television. Although Terry was gone, Canadians continued to honour him. A mountain in British Columbia was named after him. Terry was **inducted** into the Sports Hall of Fame. In 2005, a one-dollar coin was **minted** with Terry's image on it. Today, Terry still represents hope for people who live with cancer.

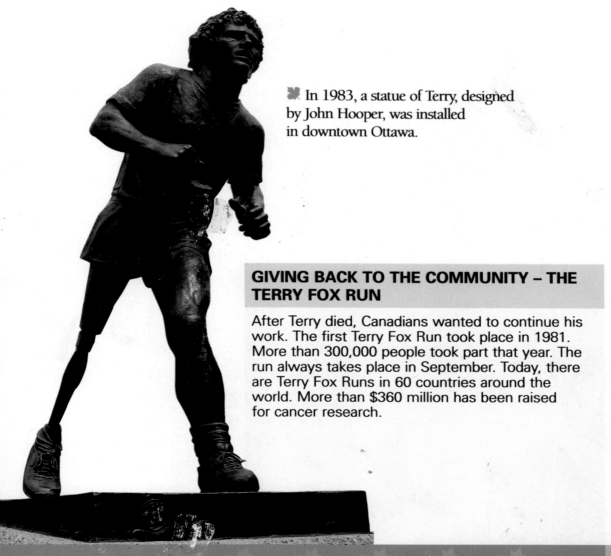

In 1983, a statue of Terry, designed by John Hooper, was installed in downtown Ottawa.

GIVING BACK TO THE COMMUNITY – THE TERRY FOX RUN

After Terry died, Canadians wanted to continue his work. The first Terry Fox Run took place in 1981. More than 300,000 people took part that year. The run always takes place in September. Today, there are Terry Fox Runs in 60 countries around the world. More than $360 million has been raised for cancer research.

Write a Biography

Some people have very interesting lives. They may overcome problems or achieve great success. A person's life story can be the subject of a book. This kind of a book is called a biography. There are many biographies in a library. The biographies describe the lives of movie stars, athletes, and great leaders. These people may be alive today, or they may have lived many years ago. Reading a biography can help you learn more about a person.

At school, you might be asked to write a biography review. First, decide who you want to write about. You can choose a health hero, such as Terry Fox, or any other person you find interesting. Then, find out if your library has any books about this person. Learn as much as you can about him or her. Write down the key events in this person's life. What was this person's childhood like? What has he or she accomplished? What are his or her goals? What makes this person special or unusual?

A concept web is a useful research tool. Read the questions in the following concept web. Answer the questions in your notebook. Your answers will help you write your biography review.

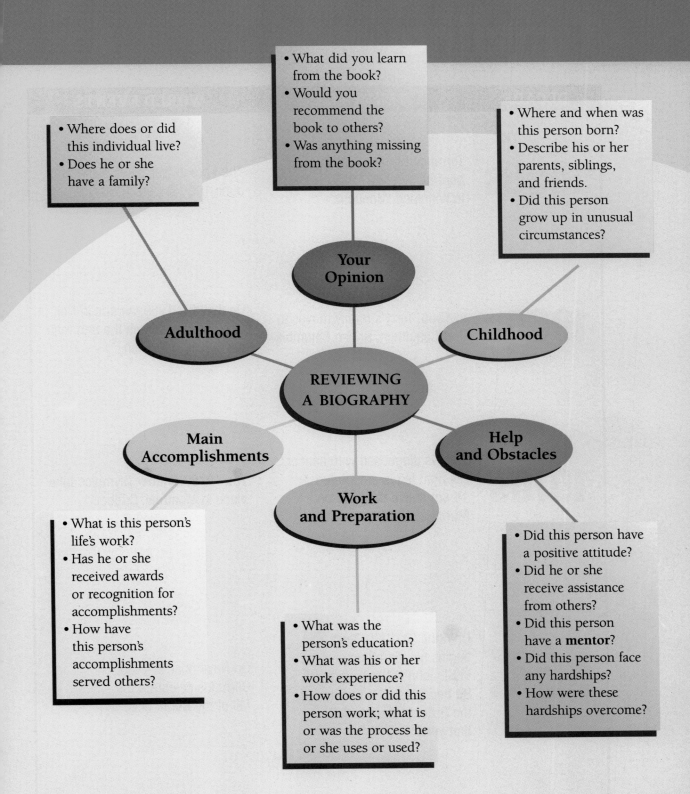

- Where does or did this individual live?
- Does he or she have a family?

- What did you learn from the book?
- Would you recommend the book to others?
- Was anything missing from the book?

- Where and when was this person born?
- Describe his or her parents, siblings, and friends.
- Did this person grow up in unusual circumstances?

Your Opinion

Adulthood

Childhood

REVIEWING A BIOGRAPHY

Main Accomplishments

Help and Obstacles

Work and Preparation

- What is this person's life's work?
- Has he or she received awards or recognition for accomplishments?
- How have this person's accomplishments served others?

- What was the person's education?
- What was his or her work experience?
- How does or did this person work; what is or was the process he or she uses or used?

- Did this person have a positive attitude?
- Did he or she receive assistance from others?
- Did this person have a **mentor**?
- Did this person face any hardships?
- How were these hardships overcome?

Timeline

DECADE	TERRY FOX	WORLD EVENTS
1950s	Terrance Stanley Fox is born on July 28, 1958, in Winnipeg, Manitoba.	The Korean War takes place from June 1950 to July 1953.
1960s	In 1966, Terry's family moves to Port Coquitlam, British Columbia.	On July 21, 1969, American Neil Armstrong becomes the first man to walk on the moon.
1970s	Terry is diagnosed with cancer. His right leg is amputated 15 cm above the knee on March 9, 1977.	The 1976 Summer Olympics take place in Montreal, Quebec.
1980s	On April 12, 1980, Terry begins his Marathon of Hope in St. John's, Newfoundland. He becomes a Companion of the Order of Canada later that year.	On November 9, 1989, Germans celebrate the fall of the Berlin Wall.

Further Research

How can I find out more about Terry Fox?

Most libraries have computers that connect to a database for searching for information. If you input a key word, you will be provided with a list of books in the library that contain information on that topic. Non-fiction books are arranged numerically, using their call number. Fiction books are organized alphabetically by the author's last name.

Websites

To learn more about Terry Fox, visit:
www.collectionscanada.ca/2/6/h6-214-e.html

To see a list of the top 10 Greatest Canadians, including Terry Fox, visit:
CBC www.cbc.ca/greatest

Words to Know

amputated: when a body part is removed during an operation

artificial: made by people

chemotherapy: a kind of cancer treatment that uses drugs or chemicals to destroy the cancer

disabilities: the lack of certain abilities

donations: gifts of money

fibreglass: glass spun into fine threads or fibres

funeral: a ceremony to remember a person who has died

inducted: became a member

inspiration: the power to influence someone to do something

kinesiology: the study of movement

marathon: a long-distance run of 42,195 metres

mentor: a wise and trusted teacher

minted: created coins or bills

obstacles: things that stand in the way of progress

Parkinson's disease: a chemical imbalance in the brain that, over time, makes it difficult or impossible to move certain parts of the body

prosthetic: an artificial body part

spinal cord: a thick cord of nerves that runs down the spine and controls feeling and movement throughout the body

Index